Table of Contents

I0170512

Recipes with Nuts and Seeds

Tasty nuts and seeds food ideas to step up your food game

BY: Ida Smith

License Notes

This book is licensed for your personal enjoyment only. This book may not be re-sold or given away to other people. If you would like to share this book with another person, please purchase an additional copy for each recipient. If you're reading this book and did not purchase it, or it was not purchased for your use only, then please return to your favorite ebook retailer and purchase your own copy. Thank you for respecting the hard work of this author.

Introduction

Nothing sucks like staying at a loss of recipe ideas when you know fun nuts recipes is all you need to make breakfast, lunch, and dinner time a memorable moment. If you have children or an elderly staying with you, then you don't have to bore anyone anymore with the same nuts and seeds recipes. Try something new and incredible this year and give your family a meal time they will always look forward to.

Smart and Healthy Raisin Cereal Bowl

Breakfast is always a delight when raisin cereal makes the day's menu. And if you are craving a healthy touch, here is a recipe to love and cherish.

Ingredient List:

- 1 cup. almond milk or coconut milk
- 1 cup. organic grain cereal
- 4 tbsp. raisins
- ½ tsp cinnamon
- 1tbsp chopped apples

Preparation:
In a large bowl, combine cereal, raisins, cinnamon, apples, and mix
Pour milk over the content and serve

Have a swell breakfast time!

Preparation Time: 5 minutes
Additional time: 2 minutes
Total time: 7 minutes
Makes: 3 servings

Flaxseed Bread

Bread is a perfect way to start the day and if you dread gluten, here is a tasty and healthy option for you.

Ingredient List:

- 3 cups gluten-free flour
- baking soda
- sea salt
- baking powder
- ½ cup almond milk
- ½ cup Flax seeds, divided
- ½ cup Chia seeds, divided
- ½ cup Sesame seeds, divided

Preparation:

Preheat oven to 360 degrees

Combine all dry ingredients in a bowl

Pour in the milk, stir well to make a dough

Turn it over on a floured surface, work for a while, and place dough inside the ready paper-lined baking pan

Paint the top with milk and drizzle the seeds over it

Bake for 55 minutes, remove from the heat and leave for cooling

Slice and serve with favorite tea or drink

Enjoy!

Preparation Time: 20 minutes

Cook time: 55 minutes

Total time: 1 hour 15 minutes Yields 1 loaf

Nutty Cauliflower Burst

Cauliflowers are loved for the healthy colors they decorate our health with. And if you are looking for a stylish twist to it, you have one before you.

Ingredient List:

- 1/2 head of cauliflower
- fish sauce
- ½ cup peanut butter, chunky
- lemon juice
- 1 cup breadcrumbs
- Thai chili
- ½ tsp ginger powder
- ½ cup. water
- Minced green onions for serving

– Sriracha and cilantro for serving too

Preparation:

Preheat oven to 360 degrees

Cut cauliflower into halves, remove the core and cut into big florets

In a clean bowl, mix peanut butter, water, chili, fish sauce, lemon juice, and ginger

In another bowl spread the panko, you can toast it lightly for more crunchiness if you like

Dip each floret in the peanut mixture and toss it over the panko. Place the coated floret on the baking tray, repeat same for others, and slide the tray into the oven

Bake for 35 minutes, remove from the heat, garnish with the Sriracha, cilantro, and green onions

Serve with joy!

Preparation Time: 20 minutes

Cook time: 35 minutes

Total time: 55 minutes

Makes: 5 servings

Easy Banana Flax Seed Crepes

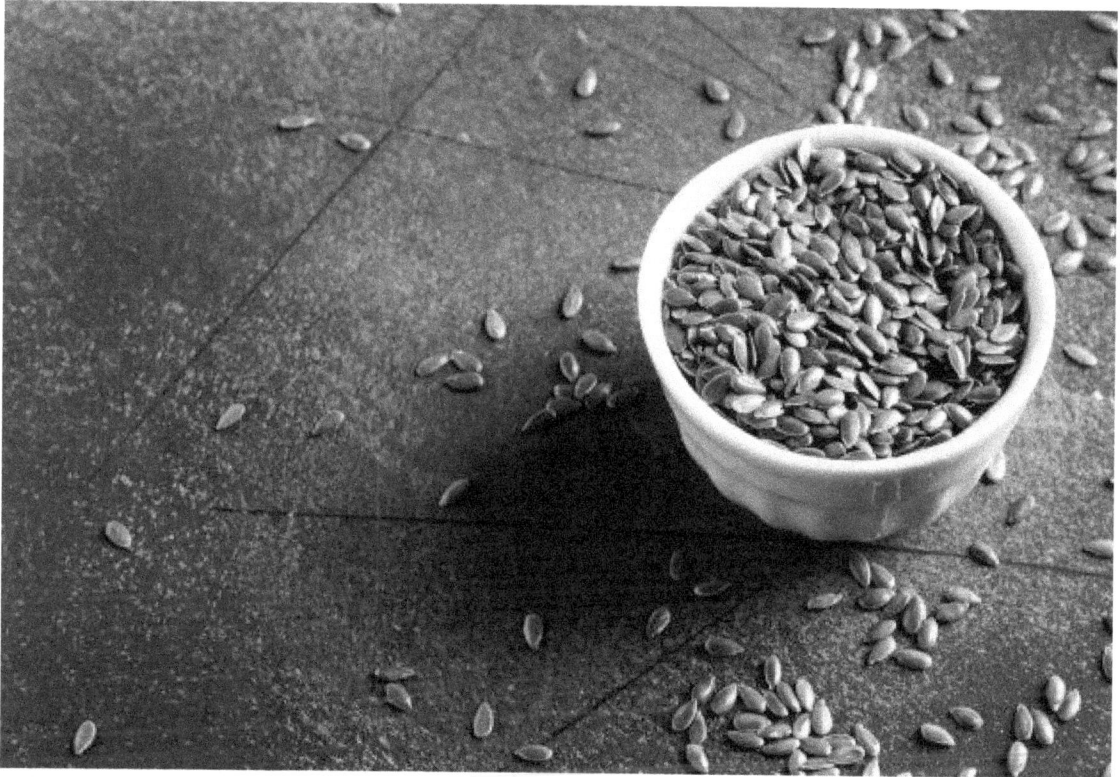

Have you ever wondered how flaxseed taste in pancakes? Well, here your permission to explore and indulge.

Ingredient List:

- 2 overripe bananas, mashed
- 4 large eggs
- cinnamon powder
- flax seeds
- baking powder
- 1 ½ tbsp. butter

Preparation:

In a large bowl, combine the mashed banana, flax seeds, cinnamon, eggs, and baking powder. Mix to incorporation

Melt butter in a large nonstick saucepan, scoop batter into the pan, and cook till it bubbles and forms a round firm crepe. Flip over to cook through, transfer to a platter.

Cook remaining batter same, leave for cooling and serve with maple syrup if needed

Enjoy!

Preparation Time: 15 minutes

Cook time: 30 minutes

Total time: 45 minutes

Makes: 12 servings

Choco-Banana And Coco-Muffins

For the love of chocolate and coconut, you can try your hands on this easy and tasty muffin twist. It's a new year, so you are free to explore fun nuts and seed recipes.

Ingredient List:

- 4 large eggs
- 1 cup. coconut powder
- 3 ripe bananas
- 1 cup. Greek yogurt
- ½ cup white sugar
- A pinch of salt
- ½ tsp vanilla extract
- ½ tsp cinnamon powder
- 1 cup dark chocolate, roughly chopped

– ½ tsp. baking soda

Preparation:

Preheat oven to 320 degrees and prepare your muffin tray with parchment paper

Whisk bananas, yogurt, sugar, and vanilla in a bowl

Fold in the other ingredients except for the chocolate. Stir well to incorporate, add half of the chocolate chips, and pour batter into muffin pans

Top each filled muffin compartment with the remaining chocolate chips and bake in the oven for 35 minutes

Remove from the heat, set aside for cooling, and serve

Have a blast!

Preparation Time: 20 minutes

Cook time: 35 minutes

Total time: 55 minutes

Makes: 15 servings

Seedy And Nuts Porridge

Here is a quick, easy, and delicious breakfast idea that is perfect for you and your family.

Ingredient List:

- 2 cups Walnuts
- 2 ½ cups Milk
- 2 cups almond seeds
- ½ cup chia seeds
- 1 cup coconut flakes
- 1 cup date syrup or honey
- 1 cup sunflower seeds
- kosher salt
- flaxseed
- hemp seed
- cinnamon powder

– sesame seeds

Preparation:

In a large clean bowl, throw in all ingredients

Mix well to incorporate and seal the lid of the bowl (microwave safe) with a plastic cover

Sit content in the refrigerator for 7 hours or overnight

In the morning, microwave it for 3 minutes, spoon into plates

Garnish with favorite fruits and serve

Enjoy the yummy blast!

Preparation Time: 15 minutes

Freezing time: 7 hours

Total time: 7 hours 15 minutes

Makes: 5 servings

Avocado Sesame Wrap

It's sushi lunchtime and avocado have come to dine, so grab an apron and make magic with sesame seeds.

Ingredient List:

- 1 English cucumber, sliced
- 1 avocado, boldly sliced
- Seaweed, toasted
- 1 cup sesame seeds

Preparation:
Lay the seaweed on a platter
Top it with the cucumber and avocado slices
Drizzle the seeds over it and roll to a bundle
Serve with love!

Preparation Time: 10 minutes
Additional time: 5 minutes
Total time: 15 minutes
Makes: 5 servings

Gluten-Free Green Matcha Pancakes

Love nuts but scared of gluten? Here is a healthy option with the best green tea to step up your breakfast game and have a blissful day.

Ingredient List:

- matcha green tea powder
- 2 ½ cups Brown rice flour
- sugar
- 3tbsp hemp protein powder
- 1 ½ tsp. baking powder
- 2 large eggs
- sunflower oil or coconut oil
- butter

Toppings

- 1 ½ Greek yogurt
- ½ cup almonds seeds
- ½ cup chia seeds
- ½ cup walnuts
- ½ cup dried fruits and raisins
- 1 cup maple syrup
- ½ cup. cocoa powder
- coconut oil

Preparation:

In a big clean bowl, whisk the sugar, egg, milk, and coconut oil or sunflower oil together.

Fold in the rice flour, matcha, baking powder, and hemp powder. Mix well to blend.

Melt the butter in a clean large nonstick skillet and scoop in the batter. Cook till it forms while flipping from side to side. Transfer to a platter when cooked through and repeat the process for the remaining batter.

In a small bowl, mix the yogurt, seeds, and nuts.

In a separate bowl, mix the maple syrup, coconut oil, and cocoa powder to make a syrup.

Arrange the ready pancakes in a flat plate or platter, top it with the yogurt and nuts mixture followed by the chocolate syrup

Serve with your favorite smoothie or juice

Have fun!

Preparation Time: 30 minutes

Cook time: 30 minutes

Total time: 1 hour

Makes: 12 servings

Seedy Nut Butter

Sometimes, trying stuff all by yourself gives a good feeling of accomplishment. Well, if you dislike store-bought peanut butter, here is a recipe you can make and be proud of yourself.

Ingredient List:

- 1 cup mixed nuts of almond, groundnuts, and other preferred
- 1/2 cup chia seeds
- 1/2 cup sesame seeds
- 1/2 cup pumpkin seeds
- ½ tsp. sea salt
- olive oil or coconut oil

Preparation:
Pour nuts, salt, and seeds into the food processor and pulse till nuts are broken down

Add the oil and keep pulsing, use a spatula to scrape content splashed on the processor down

Empty content into a sterilized jar, cover, and store in the refrigerator

Use as a spread on your bread, crackers, etc.

Enjoy!

Preparation Time: 10 minutes

Additional time: 5 minutes

Total time: 15 minutes

Makes: 2 jars

Chia-Pumpkin Pudding

Chia seeds are one of the most loved seeds, all thanks to the astounding health benefits they supply. And when matched with vitamin-filled pumpkin, you are promised a super lunch to keep you energized the entire afternoon.

Ingredient List:

- 2cups Milk
- 1 cup chia seeds
- 2cups pumpkin puree
- pumpkin spice
- ½ cup maple syrup or date syrup

Toppings

- ½ cup fresh blueberries

- ½ cup sunflower seeds
- ½ cup almonds, sliced
- ¼ cup dried fruits (optional)

Preparation:

In a clean bowl, toss in all the ingredients and mix well to blend.

Store in the refrigerator for 1 hour.

Remove from chilling and serve.

Enjoy while in the car or the office.

Preparation Time: 20 minutes

Freezing time: 1 hour

Total time: 1 hour 20 minutes

Makes: 7 servings

Corny Caramel Mix

Do you have movie time with your family in the evening? Ditch the popcorn and make your family proud.

Ingredient List:

- 1 cup almonds
- 1 cup butter
- 1 cup brown sugar
- 1 ¼ cups pecans
- 1 cup white corn syrup
- 1 (14 ounces) crispy corn and rice cereal

Preparation:
Preheat oven to 200 degrees

In a microwave-safe bowl, combine sugar, butter, and corn syrup. Microwave it for 3 minutes or till the butter melts

Pour cereal, almonds, pecans into the prepared baking tray/pan

Pour butter mixture over it and stir well to blend

Bake in the oven for 1 hour, stirring frequently to prevent lumps

Serve with a favorite drink when cooled

Have fun!

Preparation Time: 20 minutes

Cook time: 1 hour

Total time: 1 hour 20 minutes

Makes: 20 servings

Vegan Seedy Smoothie

Smoothie goes well with some slices of toast or biscuits for dinner, and if you love the idea of a vegan burst, here is a recipe to try.

Ingredient List:

- 2 frozen bananas
- 2tsp hemp protein powder
- 3 cups Almond, cashew, or tiger nut milk
- 3 tsp. organic spirulina powder
- 1oz mint leave

Toppings

- Chia seeds

– Hemp heart

Preparation:
Toss all ingredient into your blender and pulse to a smooth puree.
Pour into jars and garnish with toppings.
Serve with delight!
Preparation Time: 15 minutes
Additional time: 5 minutes
Total time: 20 minutes
Makes: 4 servings

Oatsy Pear And Almond Crumble

Lunch is fun when oats meet almonds in this delicious crumble, giving you the lingering sweetness pear is known for.

Ingredient List:

- 2 cups Rolled oats
- 1 cup brown sugar, divided
- ¾ cup white flour
- 1 cup butter, soften
- 2 cups pears, peeled and diced
- ½ tsp. cinnamon powder
- 2 ¼ cups peeled and finely diced apples
- 1 cup almonds

Preparation:

Preheat oven to 300 degrees

In a large bowl, combine oats, ½ cup of sugar, butter, flour to a fine mix

In a separate bowl, mix remaining sugar, cinnamon, apples, pears, to a fine blend and spread content on the base of the pan

Top it with the oats mixture and almonds

Bake in the oven for 45 minutes or till the surface is lightly tanned

Remove from the heat and serve with love.

Have fun!

Preparation Time: 15 minutes

Cook time: 45 minutes

Total time: 1 hour

Makes: 10 servings

Organic Protein Goodness

What a world of protein, what a world of good! Inspired taste buds, healthy treats, and more are the promises from this bowl of protein goodness. So, you can plan for a good lunchtime.

Ingredient List:

– 1 cup whey protein powder
– 3 cups almond milk
– organic Acai powder
– 2 ripe bananas
– 3cups Strawberries, frozen

Toppings

– Granola

- Chia seeds
- Fresh fruits
- Bananas
- Strawberries
- Mangoes

Preparation:

Pour all ingredients except the topping s into the food processor and pulse till desire consistency is achieved

Pour content into bowls and garnish with toppings

Serve with joy!

Preparation Time: 20 minutes

Additional time: 5 minutes

Total time: 25 minutes

Makes: 6 servings

Vanilla Almond Waffles

Excite your taste buds with this tasty treat of waffles. If you are looking for a simple and easy breakfast or a light evening treat, don't go far, try this out and be proud of your creation.

Ingredient List:

- 3 large eggs
- 1 cup almond flour
- A pinch of salt
- ¼ cup honey or maple syrup
- baking powder
- vanilla extract
- almonds, roughly chopped

Preparation:

Preheat the waffle iron

In a large bowl, fold in the almond flour, salt, and baking powder

In another small bowl, beat the egg, vanilla, and honey.

Make a hole in the floured bowl, pour egg mixture into it, and mix

Spray the cooking spray over the waffle iron, pour mixed batter into the hot iron, cook till well-tanned

Serve warm with delight!

Preparation Time: 15 minutes

Cook time: 12 minutes

Total time: 27 minutes

Makes: 7 servings

Dairy-Free Healthy Bars

Granola bars are one of the healthiest forms of on the go meals that guarantees tons of goodness. And if you are scared of dairy misgivings, here is a free choice for your delight.

Ingredient List:

- 1 cup organic peanut butter
- 1 cup rolled oats
- 1 cup cashew, roughly chopped
- ½ cup dried strawberries
- 1/3 cup raw sunflower seeds
- 1 cup mulberries, dried and chopped
- 2 large ripe bananas, mashed
- organic hemp protein powder
- chia seeds

Preparation:

Preheat oven to 300 degrees

Whisk peanut butter with the banana in a bowl

Fold in other ingredients in succession, mixing to a well-incorporated form

Pour batter into your prepared baking tray and bake for 35 minutes

Remove from the heat and leave for cooling

Cut granola into bars, stuff in your lunch box, and preserve leftover in the freezer for later

Have fun on the go!

Preparation Time: 25 minutes

Cook time: 35 minutes

Total time: 1 hour

Makes: 14 bars

Cinna-Candied Almonds

Almonds are forever! Says a happy dad who carelessly flaunts his almond addiction. So, if you have anyone with a strong craving for almonds, keep them close to your heart with this recipe.

Ingredient List:

- 3 cups. Almonds, whole
- 1 cup. sugar
- 1 cup. water
- 1 ½ tbsp. fresh ground cinnamon

Preparation:

Mix the water, cinnamon, and sugar in a clean saucepan and cook over moderate heat
Add almonds and cook till liquid evaporates, giving a syrup coating on the almonds
Drain almonds on a baking sheet, taking care to separate with a fork. Leave it to cool before serving
Have a fun-filled dinner!
Preparation Time: 10 minutes
Cook time: 20 minutes

Total time: 30 minutes
Makes: 4 servings

Nutzy Banana Bread

Banana is a whole bundle of goodness and vitality and the thought of infusing its renowned sweetness into loaves, hands you a healthful crunch in every bite.

Ingredient List:

- 5 overripe bananas, mashed
- 3 large eggs
- 1cup honey
- 1 cup. coconut oil
- ½ cup applesauce
- ½ cup milk
- 1tsp cinnamon powder
- 1tsp vanilla extract
- 4 cups white flour

- ½ cup rolled oats
- 1tsp baking soda
- 1 1/2 tsp baking powder

Toppings

- ½ cup walnuts, chopped
- Granola
- Dried fruits
- Coconut flakes
- Chia seeds

Preparation:

Preheat oven to 300 degrees, prepare baking pan, and leave aside

In a large bowl, mix all ingredients except the toppings together. When well mixed, pour batter into the ready baking pan and bake for 1 hour or till the tester comes out clean

Remove from the heat and allow cooling inside the pan for 5 minutes

Transfer to the wire rack, slice, and serve when completely cooled

Have a fun-filled mealtime!

Preparation Time: 20 minutes

Cook time: 1 hour

Total time: 1 hour 20 minutes

Makes: 15 servings

Buttery Flax Seed Cookies

Still on flaxseed, here is a rich, tasty, and easy cookie recipe to make for dinner. And you will never love a seedless cookie again.

Ingredient List:

- 1 cup coconut flour
- 1 ½ cups peanut butter
- 1 cup flax seed meal
- baking powder
- vanilla extract
- 3 eggs
- ½ cup applesauce, unsweetened
- ½ cup butter, melted

Preparation:

Preheat oven to 360 degrees

Combine the flaxseed, vanilla extract, baking powder, salt, coconut flour in a large bowl

Mix the applesauce, peanut butter in a small bowl before pouring it into the dry content.

Make a dough, cut it into balls, flatten them, and place on a baking sheet

Bake for 20 minutes, turn off the heat, leave it on the wired rack for cooling

Serve with love!

Preparation Time: 15 minutes

Cook time: 20 minutes

Total time: 35 minutes

Makes: 14 servings

Seedy Cauliflower Delight

How do you like your cauliflower? In salads only? Wait till you have tried this yumminess, you will never eat a bland salad again.

Ingredient List:

- ½ head of cauliflower
- 2 ¼ tsp miso paste
- sesame oil
- rice vinegar
- ½ cup honey
- ½ tsp. granulated garlic
- black sesame seeds for serving
- Chopped cilantro for serving too

Preparation:

Preheat oven to 380 degrees

Dress cauliflower, cut into halves, remove the core, and cut into florets

In a clean bowl, mix the honey, miso, vinegar, sesame oil, water, and garlic.

Dip each floret in the honey mixture, place on a prepared baking tray, drizzle the sesame seeds over them, and bake for 25 minutes or till florets are sticky

Transfer to a platter and serve with cilantro

Have a blast!

Preparation Time: 20 minutes

Cook time: 25 minutes

Total time: 45 minutes

Makes: 5 servings

Easy Buckeyes For Winter

Do you have little ones or would you fancy super tasty and east to make a chocolate-inspired nutty snack? Here is a recipe to hold dearly.

Ingredient List:

- 5 cups chocolate chips
- 1 cup butter, soften
- 2 cups peanut butter, crunchy
- vanilla extract
- 7 cups confectioner's sugar

Preparation:

Combine sugar, vanilla, peanut butter, and butter in a bowl to make a dough
Cut out dough into small round balls and arrange them on a paper-lined baking tray
Place a toothpick above each ball and slide the tray into the freezer. Sit it there for 35 minutes

Melt the chocolate chips in a double boiler, stirring till well blended

Remove frozen butter and dip in the chocolate content, leave some part of the butterball uncovered to give it a buckeye. Return to the freezer and chill till you are ready to serve

Have fun!

Preparation Time: 25 minutes

Cook time: 10 minutes

Freezing time: 45 minutes

Total time: 1 hour 20 minutes

Makes: 10 servings

Moringa Oatmeal Porridge

This tropical tree goodness of moringa has been making the headlines for amazing health offerings. If you didn't know what oats could do with it, here is the recipe you need.

Ingredient List:

- 3 cups rolled oats
- 4 cups milk of choice
- moringa powder
- maple syrup
- vanilla extract
- cinnamon powder
- ½ coconut shreds
- 1/2 cup chopped pistachios
- chia seeds

– ½ cup mulberries, dried

Preparation:

Over moderate heat, in a clean saucepan, stir in the oats, maple syrup, milk, vanilla, cinnamon, and sauté

Stirring occasionally till oats is completely absorbed and soften

Turn off the heat, stir in the moringa powder and remaining ingredients

Spoon into plates and serve

Have fun!

Preparation Time: 10 minutes

Cook time: 10 minutes

Total time: 20 minutes

Makes: 5 servings

Buttery Peanut Fudge

A buttery bite is the best thing to happen during lunch that everyone will love. Here is another toast to a lunch of buttery sensation.

Ingredient List:

- ½ cup peanut butter, crunchy style
- ½ cup butter
- ½ cup milk, any kind
- 1 (6 ounces) brown sugar
- 3 cups Confectioners' sugar
- vanilla extract
- ½ tsp. cinnamon (optional)
- ¼ cup walnuts or almonds, chopped

Preparation:

Over moderate heat, melt the butter in a skillet, whisk in the milk, and brown sugar. Stirring occasionally for 3 minutes, turn off the heat

Fold in the peanut butter, and vanilla, and pour in over the confectioner's sugar. Mix well to incorporate and pour content into a paper-lined bowl

Transfer to the refrigerator and chill for 2 hours or till it forms a firm bar

Cut into bars and serve

Have a blast!

N/B: loosen the confectioner's sugar with an electric mixer for an easy blend

Preparation Time: 16 minutes

Cooking time: 5 minutes

Freezing time: 2 hours

Total time: 2 hours 21 minutes

Makes: 16 servings

Cheesy Cashew Potato Toast

How about potato toast? Yes, it is a promise of delight when matched with nuts and seeds. So, feel free to indulge and have a tasty evening meal.

Ingredient List:

- ½ tsp paprika, smoked
- 1 cup cashew, soaked for 4 hours in the refrigerator
- yeast
- sea salt
- 1tsp white pepper
- miso paste

Pears

- 4 bosc pears

- fresh lemon juice
- 3 cups of water
- ¼ tsp. cinnamon powder
- 3 ginger slices
- 32 thyme sprigs
- canola oil for frying
- Slices of sourdough bread for the base

Preparation:
Drain the cashew and blend it with lemon juice, salt, miso paste, yeast, white pepper, paprika. Empty content into a jar, cover, and store in the refrigerator

To poach the pear, combine water, lemon juice, sugar, cinnamon, and ginger. Boil it over the heat

Peel pears, remove the seeds, cut into halves, and place in the boiling liquid to poach for 15 minutes

Drain the pears, allow to cool, and slice thinly

Fry the thyme with the oil and set aside

Layout the sourdough slices, spread the cashew cream over them, top with pear slice and fried thyme sprigs

Serve with love!

Preparation Time: 30 minutes
Cook time: 20 minutes
Additional time: 10 minutes
Total time: 1 hour
Makes: 13 servings

Cinnamon Pecan Sandies Of Sweetness

Looking for a supreme feeling of pecans? Try your hands on this dish and you will love it!

Preparation:

- 1 cup butter
- 2 cups white flour
- ¾ cup granulated sugar
- 1tsp cinnamon powder
- ½ tsp vanilla extract
- water
- 1 cup pecans
- ¼ tsp. kosher salt

Preparation:

Preheat oven to 300 degrees

Whisk butter and sugar in a stand mixer till light and creamy

Fold in the water, vanilla, and salt

Add flour, resume mixing till well blended. Toss in the pecans and mix to incorporate

Scoop mixture into round balls, flatten with your palms and lay them on the baking tray

Bake for 15 minutes, allow cooling before you serve

Have fun!

Preparation Time: 25 minutes

Cook time: 15 minutes

Total time: 40 minutes

Makes: 12 servings

Rainbow Salsa

A beautiful and tasty bowl of salad is one of the best dinners to end the day with. And if you fancy a colorful dish, here is a recipe to discover.

Ingredient List:

- 1 cup rainbow quinoa. cooked
- 1 ¼ cups frozen and thawed corn
- 2 large avocados, nicely diced
- 10 cup romaine lettuce, roughly chopped
- 1 can black beans, well-drained and rinsed
- 1 cup tomatoes, diced
- ½ cup red onions, nicely diced
- ½ cup cilantro, finely chopped
- lemon juice, fresh

– Any dressing you desire

Preparation:

Lay the lettuce in a bowl, add the quinoa, beans, tomato, lemon juice, cilantro, onions, avocado, corn, and drizzle the dressing over it

Serve with delight!

Preparation Time: 15 minutes

Additional time 5 minutes

Total time: 20 minutes

Makes: 4 servings

Blueberries Pecan Energy Balls

Do you fancy a smart lunch you can crunch on your way back to work on a busy day? You need energy balls. You need all the strength you can get while working and these tasty nutty bites are a handful too.

Ingredient List:

- 2 cups Pecans
- 7 tbsp. peanut or almond butter
- 2 cups dried blueberries
- cocoa nibs
- chia seeds
- ½ tsp. sea salt
- maple syrup

Preparation:

Toss the chia seeds, blueberries, pecans, cocoa nibs, butter, and maple syrup into the food processor. Pulse for 25 minutes or till finely crushed

Wet your hands, scoop mixture, and make a round sturdy ball

Store in the refrigerator and take out when ready to eat

Serve with love!

Preparation Time: 20 minutes

Additional time: 5 minutes

Makes: 6 servings

Oats And Fruits Bowl (Slow-Cooker)

What a wonderful bowl of oats supreme for lunch! If you are lost for ideas to spark the life of oats in your pantry, here is a vow to sweetness.

Ingredient List:

- − 2 1/4 cups Steel-cut oats
- − 1 cup pitted dates, chopped
- − kosher salt
- − ¼ tsp. cinnamon powder
- − 1 cup milk
- − 1cup cranberries, dried
- − ½ cup honey
- − 6 cups of water
- − ½ cup chia seeds

– 1 cup walnuts or sunflower seeds

Preparation:
Fold in the oats, cinnamon, salt, water into a slow cooker and cook for 7 hours
Toss in the milk, cranberries, honey, dates.
Spoon content into bowls, garnish with walnuts and chia seeds
Serve with love!
Preparation Time: 10 minutes
Cook time: 7 hours
Total time: 7 hours 10 minutes
Makes: 4 servings

Chia Blueberries Overnight Pudding

One of the best ways to start your morning or end your day is having a bowl of delicious pudding and chia seeds seems a perfect match for the task.

Ingredient List:

- 3 tbsp. chia seeds
- ½ tsp. almond extract
- ½ cup. coconut milk
- 3tbsp maple syrup
- toasted almonds, chopped
- 1 cup fresh blueberries

Preparation:

Combine the milk, maple syrup, almond extract, and chia in a bowl. Sit content in the refrigerator for 7 hours or overnight or 2 days

When needed, spoon pudding into a microwave bowl, heat it for 2 minutes, top with blueberries, almonds, and dried/fresh fruits (if desired)

Serve with love!

Preparation Time: 15 minutes

Freezing time: 7 hours

Total time: 7 hours 15 minutes

Makes: 4 servings

Seedy Salmon Tart

Salmons are not just tasty, but they are made for your heart's health, and the addition of pumpkin seeds promises all the delight and healthiness your life deserves.

Ingredient List:

- 4 (4 ounces) frozen and thawed salmon fillets
- pumpkin pie spice
- 7 saltine crackers, crushed
- 2 carrots, cut diagonally
- ½ tsp. kosher salt
- ½ cup maple syrup. Divided
- salted and roasted pumpkin seeds

Preparation:

Preheat oven to 300 degrees

Mix carrot dices with 3tbsp. maple syrup, salt, and pumpkin pie spice. Lay them out on a baking tray and bake for 12 minutes

Rinse and pat dry the salmon

In a small bowl, combine the salt, crackers, and pumpkin seed, set aside

Brush the fish with the maple syrup or date syrup (if using), drizzle the cracker mixture over them, and place them beside the carrots in the baking tray

Spray some cooking spray over the fish or drizzle coconut oil if you have and bake for 20 minutes

Remove from the heat, set to cool, garnish with pumpkin seeds, and serve

Have fun!

Preparation Time: 20 minutes

Cook time: 32 minutes

Total time: 52 minutes

Makes: 5 servings

Conclusion

Nuts and seeds are one of the most staple food items in everyone's pantry but sometimes, having the grandest idea of incorporating them in dishes may fail one. That is why these 30 super recipes cookbook is incredible and from now, you can ditch the bland old-fashioned style your hands are accustomed to and invent extraordinary dishes.

Don't miss out!

Visit the website below and you can sign up to receive emails whenever Ida Smith publishes a new book. There's no charge and no obligation.

https://books2read.com/r/B-A-LRXL-CELLB

BOOKS 2 READ

Connecting independent readers to independent writers.

www.ingramcontent.com/pod-product-compliance
Lightning Source LLC
Chambersburg PA
CBHW081301040426
42452CB00014B/2593